NON-LINEAR EDITING

A Survey

CHRIS THOMPSON

S K I L L S E T

THE INDUSTRY TRAINING ORGANISATION FOR BROADCAST, FILM & VIDEO

BRITISH FILM INSTITUTE

bfi

BFI PUBLISHING

First published in 1994 by the
British Film Institute
21 Stephen Street
London W1P 1PL

The British Film Institute exists to encourage the development of film, television and video in the United Kingdom, and to promote knowledge, understanding and enjoyment of the culture of the moving image. Its activities include the National Film and Television Archive; the National Film Theatre; the Museum of the Moving Image; the London Film Festival; the production and distribution of film and video; funding and support for regional activities; Library and Information Services; Stills, Posters and Designs; Research; Publishing and Education; and the monthly *Sight and Sound* magazine.

British Library Cataloguing in Publication Data.
A catalogue for this book is available from the
British Library

ISBN: 0–85170–490–5

Cover by Steve Ashmore

Set in 10/11.5 pt Sabon by
D R Bungay Associates, Burghfield, Berks
and printed in Great Britain by
Jason Press, Hertford

CONTENTS

FOREWORD

Skillset is the Industry Training Organisation for Broadcast, Film and Video. One of its central roles is to develop information on employment trends and training needs in order to ensure that the industry has appropriate training arrangements in place.

Chris Thompson, a student at Ruskin College, who had previously worked as an editor and production manager in the industry, had heard of Skillset and its work. He contacted us to say he was interested in undertaking some research on the industry to present as his thesis. After discussion, we agreed that an overview of non-linear editing would be useful and facilitated introductions for Chris with various experts.

A number of people have read the work. It is in Skillset's view a starting point and the conclusions drawn are Chris's personal opinions. People who know little about non-linear editing have found it a clear and understandable introduction to a technical area. The BFI approached Skillset and Chris about its publication which we were happy to collaborate on. Our only comment would be that developments are moving so quickly in this area there is already new information to add!

Dinah Caine
Director, Skillset

PREFACE

Technological change and the long-heralded convergence between the entertainment media and the telecommunications and computer industries means that we are now faced with a very uncertain, but nevertheless exciting and potentially rewarding, future in the film and television production sectors. However, the fast-changing nature of work and of working practices in these industries means that there will be a need to redefine constantly the training regime. This series will offer critical analysis on the range of issues that these changes will entail.

One of the BFI's roles is to ensure the widest possible debate about the future of our film and television culture. We believe that a healthy moving image industry requires the continual replenishment of its skills base and welcome the opportunity to work with Skillset, the industry-led body for training in the broadcasting, film and video sectors, to publish this series.

Colin MacCabe and Richard Paterson
Research and Education Division, BFI

ACKNOWLEDGMENTS

Thanks to all those industry professionals who kindly gave their time to talk to me; to Skillset for their support; and to Margaret Riley of Focal Press, for access to specialist literature.

The Author
Chris Thompson entered the film industry in 1968 and trained as a film editor. Since 1975 he has worked as a production manager and was a founder member of the Production Managers Association. Between 1991 and 1993 he studied at Ruskin College, Oxford graduating with a Labour Studies Diploma. He is currently production manager at Catalyst Television on the 1994 series of *Gardener's World* for the BBC.

INTRODUCTION

The field of non-linear editing is so new that there is very little literature published. On 27 February 1993 the Bodleian Library did not list any publications on the subject at all and neither Blackwell's bookshop in Oxford, nor Dillons or Foyle's in London, could offer any information.

Focal Press, an imprint of Butterworth-Heinemann published *Digital Non-Linear Editing* in March 1993. This is a very detailed book, which describes the history and many technical aspects of the development of non-linear editing. The author, Thomas A. Ohanion, is the chief editor of one of the two major players in the non-linear equipment supply market. His book is very thorough about the mechanics behind the screens, but offers little information on the current state of the industry, or the likely effect of the new technology on working practices.

Michael Rubin, a very experienced American picture editor and a founder member of the American Cinema Editors' trade association has written *Non-Linear*, published by the Triad Publishing Company of Florida in June 1992. Again, this book is aimed at professional editors wishing to inform themselves about the new technology. An engaging and readable book, it provides good comparative material about the different types of machines available at the time of writing. It also provides an introduction to the concepts of non-linear editing and an extension from these principles to current editing practice and how these relate to non-linear editing. Again, it contains little comment on the effect of the new technology on the industry.

Nonlinear: A Survey from the User's Point of View, research conducted between 1 June and 1 October 1992 (London: SYPHA Consultants, November 1992), was the result of a telephone survey combined with a written questionnaire of a mixture of owners and non-owners of non-linear editing equipment. The thrust of the survey was to examine awareness of the non-linear market, reasons for a particular purchase and the likelihood of a forthcoming purchase.

Film and television trade journals are beginning to publish articles about aspects of non-linear editing, but most are concerned with the equipment manufacturers' latest releases, and assessment of these machines' performance against their predecessors' and the competition. The classified advertisement departments of the trade press have remarked on the potential of the new sector, and dedicated sections of the advertisement pages have appeared since December 1992 and now represent the largest single classified sector in *Televisual*.

Only Peter Cox writing in the BECTU trade union journal has made any attempt to think about what is happening in film and tele-vision post-production. The introduction of this new technology has profound implications for television post-production working practices in the short term and for the long-term supply of trained personnel for the sector.

With practically no published material, the only way to conduct a survey of the non-linear post-production sector of British television was by interview. I therefore identified a number of key areas in the industry, and then a leading individual within each sector:

- National broadcaster – drama;
- National broadcaster – news and current affairs;
- London post-production facility with a large commercial production clientele;
- London post-production facility with a broad mix of clientele;
- London off-line post-production facility;
- London 'boutique' post-production facility;
- Independent production company;
- Regional ITV company – one of the 'Big Five';
- Regional ITV company outside the 'Big Five';
- Regional independent post-production company;
- Non-linear editing machine manufacturer.

The interviews were conducted in each interviewee's place of work in normal business hours between the 4 February 1993 and 5 March 1993. Each interview was tape-recorded and then transcribed. The interviews lasted between forty-five and seventy minutes.

The following industry professionals kindly gave their time to talk to me:

David **Archibald**	Owner/Editor	The Edit Suite, Glasgow
Rowan Bray	Facility Manager	Inphase/Capital
Ken **Connell**	Head Post-Production	BBC News
Andrew **Coppin**	Owner/Manager	Oasis TV Facilities
Bob **Dowie**	Post-Prod. Manager	Scottish TV
Robin Imray	Ex-BBC Editor	

2

Charlie **Lennard**	Owner/Manager	Nats and Optima
Roy Lockett	Deputy Gen. Sec.	BECTU
Peter **Marshall**	Dep. Chief Engineer	Channel Four
Trevor **Morecraft**	Sales Manager	Lightworks
Keith **Oliver**	Owner/Editor	Pyramid, Cardiff
Neil **Pittaway**	Head Post-Production	BBC Network TV
Bryn **Roberts**	Facility Manager	Derwin, Cardiff
Neil **Roberts**	Owner/Editor	Motivations
Stefan Sargent	Owner/Manager	Spitfire Facilities
Phil **Stone**	Owner/Manager	VTR Post-Production
John **Surtees**	Head Post-Production	Yorkshire TV
Mike **Whittaker**	Owner/Manager	20/20 Television

A full transcript of the interview is available for names in bold type

TECHNOLOGICAL CHANGE

Many people would argue that a film or television programme is 'made' in the cutting room. The cutting room is a place where artistic decisions are finalised, and the programme honed until pace, style and delivery are as good as they can be made. Programme editing or post-production has evolved into two distinct branches. Film editing, which has remained largely unchanged for over seventy-five years, and videotape editing, a newer technology that developed into its current sophisticated form from its invention in the mid-50s. Now, technological advances in computing are enabling new systems of post-production that will involve substantial changes in working practices, business operations and the construction of film and television programmes.

Non-Linear Editing – Word Processing with Moving Pictures and Sound Recordings
It is hard to remember the modern office without word processors: a regime of mechanical tasks, elderly equipment and carbon paper, typewriter rubbers and Tippex. Computers removed the mechanical drudgery and allowed those who were writing the documents to order and express their thoughts with greater ease. So, too, with pictures. It is now as easy to move a complete edited sequence within a programme as it is to move a paragraph within a letter. To extend a scene, or match exact cuts to music beats, again a few clicks. The mechanical skills of the film and television editor will be replaced by the computer, leaving the visual judgment of the editor as the only skill. But if the computer can do all the work, the need for assistants will disappear.[1] If assistants disappear, how will the next generation of editors acquire their skills?

From the earliest days of this century, film editing has been a physical process. After the film was developed, a positive copy was sent to the cutting room. The editor would cut the picture to remove errors by the cast and physical imperfections of stock and processing. The skill developed, and directors came to rely on the creative talent of the editor to improve the structure initially envisaged, and to help smooth out the rough edges. It was done by physically cutting one section of film out and joining it to another. Unused sections of film were carefully labelled and stored so original shots could be reassembled and cut in a different way as many times as required until satisfactory. The machinery was simple and robust. Even in 1994 many editors choose to use a viewing machine the design of which remains fundamentally unchanged after seventy-five years of use. The physical nature of the job required that an editor had an assistant to move the raw material about, break it down into manageable chunks and keep track of the unused portions. This job also entailed liaising with film laboratories and special effects departments. A fundamental knowledge of the physical medium and equipment was gained while 'at the elbow' of a craftsperson. A good editor would let the assistant make simple cuts, progressing with this apprenticeship until the assistant could be trusted as an editor. Another assistant would then be taken on.

The major disadvantage to film has been the delay while it was processed. Even the fastest (but least satisfactory) methods require a wait of at least three hours, and that from a dedicated plant standing by for the material. It is more usual to wait overnight. Television programmes were initially either live or transmitted from film. The 50s saw the development of videotape recorders. Initially of poor quality and requiring protected environments for operation, the technology nevertheless developed fast. In the early days to make an edit on video meant stopping the machine, thus losing the picture, and guessing where to edit by sprinkling iron filings onto the surface of the videotape to try and discern the recorded patterns! Early videotape editors came from an engineering background, as a detailed knowledge of the equipment was necessary to make it function at all. Modern videotape editing is unrecognisably different. The machines are fast and sophisticated and are controlled by computers with an ever growing array of software that daily amazes editors and audience alike.

Videotape editing, however, has one fundamental drawback. It is a *linear* format. A selected scene is electronically marked and replayed onto a record machine. A second scene is similarly marked and copied onto the end of the first, and so on until a complete programme is assembled. A typical programme may have several hundred 'events' assembled in sequential order. An editorial judgment to alter a shot creates a problem. All the shots are assembled in a linear sequence and at varying lengths. To remove a shot will leave a blank space. Any replacement shot must be exactly the same length as that which it replaces, or spaces will be left at the beginning and end; an overlong replacement will displace segments of the shots on either side. Of course, the complete programme can be copied until the section to be adjusted is reached and adjustments then made on the new master copy. This involves a loss of quality as tape is copied to tape, and a loss of time in duplicating previous work. Programme-makers have become adept at adjusting programmes as they go along, to make pieces fit music better, inserting replacement shots at exact lengths, and so forth. In short, a linear methodology has developed over the years.

In the 80s arguments raged about the technical superiority of film over videotape, but by the end of the decade the quality difference was academic. The difference in editing methods, however, remained fundamental. Film was a non-linear method of working, and videotape was not. Film was seen as the leisurely, physical, craft approach, and videotape was the fast and tricky method. Film editing equipment was cheap but editing took time. Video editing equipment could commonly cost over £1 million for a system, and was rented by the hour. It was never said, but in video edit suites an unwritten 'That will do' hung next to the charges meter. Other editing techniques were developed to reduce the time and cost pressure, but nothing altered the linear nature of the task.

The 90s are a time of change for the film and television industries. Following the reallocation of the ITV franchises in 1992, many of the new franchise holders find themselves under intense financial pressure to reduce costs to maintain their income, in order to find the treasury levy and the franchise premium, as well as shareholders' dividends. Corporate television is also being squeezed hard. Its clients are reducing their overall spend, as well as the price per minute of each programme. Cinema is suffering from rising costs. New technology is altering most aspects of the audiovisual industry. Lightweight cameras do not need four people to operate them, and for certain applications do not need sound or lighting crew either. Videotape machinery is becoming smaller, lighter, cheaper and more powerful, and the videotape itself is similarly affected. Every new development is being examined to ascertain potential production cost savings, as well as technological and qualitative benefits. High definition television will put extra strains on the quality level and costs of programme origination.

The development of digital technology has added to this environment of change. If a still picture can be digitised or recorded as a sequence of numbers, it can then be copied without quality loss. It can also be altered by computers, stored and moved easily and reliably. Each picture, however, requires large amounts of computer memory, and moving pictures require phenomenal amounts of memory. The machines necessary for random access editing need storage devices that can access gigabytes[2] of information in real time, and from 1992 the technology became affordable to broadcasters and programme-makers.

In 1992 it was estimated that there were fewer than 1,200 non-linear editing systems worldwide,[3] and that perhaps thirty systems were in use in the United Kingdom. In early 1993, the classified advertising sections of the trade press had instituted special sections for non-linear editing facilities, and leading hire companies now offer the equipment for hire without editors and with minimal technical support or training. There are the beginnings of a huge growth in the sector.

As the technology decreases in price and increases in power, not only will non-linear editing become more common, but it will change the shape of the post-production sector of the televisual industry. For instance, in artwork and graphics, which are increasingly computer generated, it will now become an integral part of the editing process. Similarly, audio post-production, already digital and non-linear, will be incorporated into the non-linear picture room. Clients will approve their finished programmes in their own offices by a telephone connection, so that editors can work in different countries on their material.

The equipment is changing so fast that few people know what the current situation is in televisual post-production, or what the future will hold. It was my intention to survey developments by conducting interviews with key people in the industry, and to use their informed opinion to preview likely developments. It may then be possible to estimate the future shape of the televisual post-production sector and the source of skilled personnel that will be required to operate it.

Notes

1. Upon seeing a demonstration of the Lightworks non-linear machine, a sixty-year-old film editor was overheard to say, 'It's like a Steenbeck with a built-in assistant.'
2. Typically one still frame requires 900 kbytes per frame, and moving pictures require more than 1 gigabyte per minute before video signal compression!
3. Michael Rubin, *Non-Linear: A Guide to Electronic Film and Video Editing* (Florida: Triad Publishing, 1992), pp. 200-10.

WHAT IS NON-LINEAR EDITING?

Programme editing is akin to writing a book. Once the raw material has arrived in the cutting room it must be assembled into the most pleasing and logical order. Many aesthetic factors come into play including the tempo of the narrative, the effect of various juxtapositions on the whole, the addition of music, and so on. The art of postproduction!

In the earliest days of programme-making, the originating medium was film. Once processed, the editing consisted mainly of removing the physical imperfections of the film stock and the grosser errors of the cast; the remainder was then joined together in the order in which it had been shot. It quickly became apparent that if the editor did not work with the original negative but with a positive copy, any cut in the positive could simply be repaired and remade in a different place. Once all the cuts and juxtapositions had been tried, the final version would have the master negative cut to match it, and copies would be taken to show to the audience.

The process of editing developed along with the quality of the medium. By the mid-30s editing had developed into an essential part of the creation of any programme. It was, and is, a very flexible method of arranging the various ingredients of programmes. Sequences of shots can be arranged in any amount of trial assemblies. It takes a matter of moments to unpick a 'Sellotape' join, remove a whole sequence and join the other parts of the programme together again. It is as simple to insert the complete sequence at another point in the programme. Lengthen a shot? No problem – find the section that you removed from the original positive 'rushes' copy and join it back on again. Need to adjust a sequence so that the cuts sit happily with the music? Ask your assistant to get out all the relevant trims and add and subtract frames and feet until everyone is happy with the result.

This system beloved of 'craftsmen' everywhere has some significant drawbacks. The cost of film is high. A roll of 35mm film with a total running time of just over ten minutes costs £334.40; developing that length of film costs £130. Then add the cost of a positive print of that roll – £518.50. Less than eleven minutes of developed and printed film costs almost £1,000. A common ratio of useless to useful material is 10:1. Each usable minute therefore costs approximately £1,000 in stock and laboratory costs alone. Many devices are employed to keep this cost to a minimum. On the set, a log will be kept of shots that are thought to be good. All the negative will be developed, but only noted takes will be printed. Those printed will not be colour corrected avoiding costly human treatment of the material, and so on.

Another significant drawback is the time taken. Mostly, film is processed overnight. Raw material must be sent to the laboratory, and returned to the cutting room, adding to the time taken. Also, the original material is being handled, and film negative is very sensitive to the slightest damage. The medium, however, remains infinitely flexible in editing and of very high quality.

In the 50s, the Ampex Corporation of America developed the first generation of videotape recorders. With poor picture quality, and no satisfactory method of editing the resulting recordings, video was a useful device for the newly emergent television stations, but had no relevance to the art of making programmes. Programmes might be recorded during the day and transmitted at night – a significant cost saving. As electronic engineering advanced, videotape took vast strides forward in quality and malleability. By the early 70s most of the viewing public could not tell the difference between live videotape, programmes and film. Videotape stock was, and is, cheap; video editing was still a problem, however. As soon as the tape stopped running through the machines, the picture and sound disappeared. As recently as 1972 the BBC coverage of the Munich Olympics massacre was edited by stopping the videotape at approximately the right point and examining the surface of the tape to try and discern the electronic patterns of the recording. The edit was made directly in the master material, and could only be played a few times before the join came apart.

As control of the machines improved, it became possible to mark electronically the front and end sections of a piece of material, and re-record that section onto another tape. New selections could be similarly identified, and recorded onto the destination tape with ever increasing accuracy. The master material was now no longer being cut, and videotape machines rarely damaged it. Effectively, you could now try edits to see how they looked, and if not satisfactory, rerecord a new section over the unsatisfactory edit: 'You run the unedited tape through on the left-hand screen and pick out the best bits. Then you record just those onto the second tape' (Dick Francis, *Break In* (Pan Books: 1987), p. 191).

9

There were two big drawbacks to videotape editing. The machinery was very expensive, required special environments in which to run and was slow. More fundamentally, because of the technology, editing was sequential. The intended first shot in the programme had to be found and laid down first. The second shot second, and so forth. By the time a programme had been assembled, perhaps three hundred shots had been assembled sequentially. As the original tape had not *physically* been cut, it was then not possible to move a sequence in the same way as moving a film sequence. To replace one shot meant that it was necessary to transfer all the accepted programme, down as far as the intended alteration, to a new tape. Then insert the new shot, return to the original edited tape and copy across the rest. This worked well, except that every time the tape was copied it lost some quality, known as 'generation loss'. Even with the best-quality machines, it was rarely possible to allow more than three generations before the quality loss became unacceptable.

As with film, the technology has improved, and now video machines are much more robust, simple to use, powerful, accurate and fast. The latest generation are computer controlled and use digital technology to record the picture signal to a very high quality. Digital signals, like computer information, can be copied many times successfully without quality loss, so some of the major objections to video editing have disappeared. However, copying part of a completed programme, inserting one shot and then copying the remainder can only be done in 'real time', that is the physical time it takes to play the tape at normal viewing speed. Editing computers now track all the edit decisions made and can repeat them automatically. Thus an edit decision list (EDL) can be manipulated on a computer to rearrange a programme without having to copy the programme in real time. The disadvantage is that a list of numbers has no picture or sound. It is not possible to judge picture quality, programme pace or any of the myriad factors that go to make a satisfactory edit. The technology is also expensive to buy and use: 'Sitting in a half million pound edit suite trying to convince a producer to try something at ten pence a second is very difficult' (Neil Pittaway).

A direct consequence of the cost of the technology that allows video editing was the development of off-line editing – a computer-derived term to differentiate cheaper machines from the highly computerised, and therefore, 'on-line' edit suites. Off-line uses video machines, in essence little different from domestic video machines, and copies of the original material on cheap stock: 'I just say that off-line is when you're not working with the original tapes' (Bob Dowie). These much cheaper machines, controlled very simply, could assemble the programme and cut it as many times as you liked. Poor picture quality through generation loss was no longer a problem, provided you could just make out what was going on, because the EDL was keeping track of your changes of direction, and when finalised, would simply control the on-line computers to replicate the off-line but at broadcast quality. Off-line editing allowed edit decisions to be taken away from the ferociously expensive on-line suites, and to recover some of the more leisurely and considered approach to editing that was traditional in film editing.

Although such EDL list management systems represented a significant advance, videotape was still essentially a linear format. Many of those people using it had grown up through the more primitive machines. They had developed skills that allowed them to adjust programmes as they went along to avoid the time-consuming problems of remaking them, and fine tuning was effectively discouraged. The programmes produced were not bad, but perhaps not as good as they could have been.

During the 80s as computer power grew and became affordable, a generation of programme-makers began to experiment with computers, videotape and film-style editing. Many of the early systems like Ediflex were pioneered by visionaries like Francis Coppola and had banks of VHS machines, all computer controlled and containing many duplicate copies of the material being edited. In much the same way as a building with three lifts will have one at the top, one at the bottom and one in the middle to minimise waiting time, so these early systems used computers to retrieve the required material from the machine with its tape at the nearest position. These were the first generation of non-linear editors (NLE). Waiting time as the machines spooled backwards and forwards searching for the specified section was considerably reduced as no machine had far to go, and clever computer software enabled the machines to 'guess' which section the editor would want next, reducing waiting time even more. Access to any part of the material appeared to be almost instant. The picture quality, however, was poor and editing was not very accurate. Later generations of NLE used videodisc players as their sources; these provided better picture quality and fast access, but the discs were made individually from the original material and were therefore expensive. They could not be reused. For the first time, however, it was possible to access the source material very quickly, with the result that a sequence could be tried without having to record it sequentially. Edit decisions were replayed in sequence by the computer from a randomly accessed bank of players. Although unwieldy, it was a real advance. The power of video with instant replay and low origination material costs was allied with the flexibility only previously available with film.

From the late 80s everybody who saw the embryonic systems wanted to work on them. Film editors no longer despised the inflexibility of videotape, and video editors were released from their linear sequential bondage. The BBC bought an early model and Yorkshire Television invested in an Ediflex VHS system in 1989, but the major equipment manufacturers were not keen suppliers: 'We did go to the manufacturers a long time ago. I personally went to Ampex, Sony and the others and asked for non-linear years ago. They weren't interested' (Neil Pittaway). Having recently developed sophisticated linear technology, they did not want to see their investment wasted. But the pressure was becoming inexorable. Programme-makers wanted it: 'It was Producer Choice that led the editors that way' (John Surtees); 'They all have contacts in Hollywood and they come back saying we must have non-linear' (Neil Pittaway); 'Our clients are asking us for it' (Phil Stone), and in keeping with the early 'back yard' innovation traditions of the computer industry, several companies started the race to corner the non-linear editing market.

In America, AVID Technology married computer engineers with videotape professionals and engineered what is now a range of NLE systems; while in England, OLE Lightworks teamed a psychologist, a graphic systems designer and a computer animator and aimed specifically to produce a film-style interface for their machine, as the new machine's method of operation closely resembled film procedures. Another American company, EMC^2, and another British contender, Optima, make up the major players in the market today.

Using a variety of interfaces between the editor and the machine, all systems have many common factors. All use readily available computer technology as the heart of their systems, and all have a graphical user interface similar to the now common 'Windows' standard for personal computers. All require the original material to be transferred in real time onto their storage devices, which is usually some form of hard disc or magneto-optical disc. Once the material is digitised in this fashion, however, access to it is virtually instant. An edit decision does not require the selected section to be 'Sellotaped' to its neighbour, nor recorded sequentially to it. The edit decision simply asks the computer to replay the section from its database memory. The next edit is replayed directly after the first from wherever it happens to be on the storage discs, and so with the third, fourth, and so on. Adjusting an edit means simply adjusting the numbers that tell the computer where the pictures are stored. To see the adjusted edit, ask the computer to replay the sections as most recently described to it. Moving a section means asking the computer to move a group of numbers to a different section of the EDL, and it can then be replayed in that position in less time than it has taken to describe the process here. The editor is not making a programme in the physical sense that he or she has been used to in the past. The end product of a NLE session is the EDL, which is then used to recreate the programme from the master tapes in the on-line suites – a process called 'conforming'. This is now so highly automated it is called auto-conforming.

Editors without exception find non-linear editing a breakthrough in their craft. Complaints are largely about the cost of the hardware, but it is widely believed that this will come down. Large users are planning to at least double their non-linear capability. For a technology that was not widely available three years ago, the implications are staggering. The installed base of NLE systems is set to double within six to eight months from the existing customer base alone: 'We purchased our first one four months ago. The second one arrived last week. Now that we've got two Avids, maybe we'll go for a Lightworks next' (Bryn Roberts); 'We're looking at getting a third – our second is on hire to Central, they've got two of their own and ours' (Neil Roberts).

Interest from programme-makers and editors is keen. Total figures are difficult to come by, but it has been estimated that fewer than 1,800 machines of all systems had been installed worldwide between 1984 and 1992, of which Lightworks were credited with thirty (Michael Rubin, *Non-Linear*, Florida: Triad Publishing Company, 1992, pp. 190–211). 'Lightworks now claim a worldwide installed base of over 200' (Trevor Morecraft). Similarly, Avid were credited with 500 systems worldwide, and a recent trade magazine survey used a base of 243 in Europe alone (*Cuts* magazine, January 1993, p. 32).

Computer technology has only recently delivered enough power and storage for NLE to become a useful post-production tool. This power, allied with the latest in easy-to-use software has produced a system that is liked by everyone who has seen it. No one has any reservations about its use or desirability. Growth in penetration of these systems into the market is likely to be so fast and thorough that we may see the disappearance of most film cutting rooms and on-line editing suites – together with their editors and assistants – in less than ten years. The redundant equipment can be written off and the personnel can retrain simply on the new systems. However, methods of work, which have grown up over many years, that fostered a more or less structured training or apprenticeship will go, along with the old equipment. The new technology will be a producer's and editor's boon today, but where will the skilled personnel come from to operate the systems tomorrow?

THE OWNERS

The spread of non-linear editing has been fast and has reached all main television production areas. The largest single activity sector of ownership identified in a survey by SYPHA[1] is unsurprisingly video post-production facilities (see fig. 1).

Fig. 1

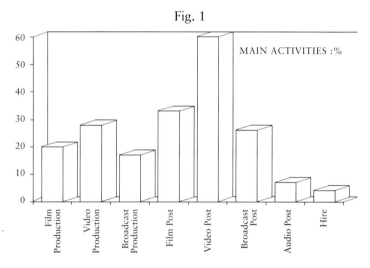

Broadcasting company post-production facilities may be under represented in the SYPHA SURVEY due to the current practice of splitting television companies into cost centres. A culture is growing in which post-production managers do not regard themselves as the final stage in an integrated process, but as profit centres and suppliers of services to customers. This will affect their descriptions of themselves in surveys: 'We are a separate division. We've got to provide resources for programme-makers' (Bob Dowie). However, it is clear that all areas of post-production are using non-linear editing, and that ancillary sectors such as audio post-production are utilising the new technology. The equipment is, however, still predominantly located in the south, with regional installations mainly in network Independent Television companies: 'I'm still the only independent non-linear system in Glasgow – the first, the original, the best' (David Archibald); 'I did a count up the other day. There's probably in the region of thirty or forty with another half-dozen in the regions' (Phil Stone).

Significantly the hire sector is a small owner of non-linear. When expensive new technology emerges, the hire sector is frequently the only sector that can guarantee sufficiently high usage to justify the high initial cost. In this case the technology is widely seen to be of such benefit that end users are buying directly, even though cost is a significant factor: 'It's a bit of a loss leader for a facility – film editors more or less have to have it these days' (Phil Stone).

If we look at the types of clients of installed systems, we see a truer reflection of the use of these machines. Eighty per cent of owners reported clients from the broadcast sector in the SYPHA survey, with the next most significant sectors being advertising agencies and corporate producers (see fig. 2).

Fig. 2

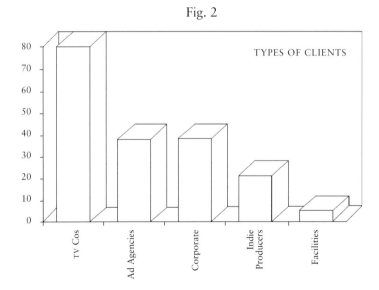

Despite some industry resistance: 'Why tamper with something that works? I've got good film editors' (Bob Dowie); 'There are a lot of facilities, broadcasters, film editors who are pretending that non-linear isn't there in the hope that it will go away' (Trevor Morecraft), it is generally seen as necessary, and a genuine advance. The television industry has a long history of seizing new technology to enhance programme-making possibilities. Non-linear editing has, however, had a much wider acceptance than some of the recent technological innovations: 'It's very, very much the way to work' (Andrew Coppin); 'We have production demand for these devices' (Neil Pittaway).

Interest in acquiring non-linear equipment started as soon as it became technologically possible, and quickly spread throughout the industry: 'We decided that we must be part of this, otherwise we'll have the editors and not the machines. Having bought it there was so much demand it became obvious that we had to buy a second one. Now they are both booked until next January' (Bryn Roberts).

This attitude is prevalent throughout the industry. There is a marked shift in opinion of both production and post-production personnel in favour of non-linear. Even the publisher-broadcasters whose attitude that 'all programmes with the exception of news would come through the door complete on tape ready for transmission' (Peter Marshall), is now being tempered by the commercial reality of the new methods of post-production: 'There probably is scope for taking a proactive not reactive approach to it' (Peter Marshall). Mainstream broadcasters responded to internal producer pressure: 'One of the reasons we got big into non-linear was because our drama producers want to play Hollywood and who can blame them. We have four Avids and four Lightworks here' (Neil Pittaway).

Facility companies were also quick to respond to the change in production attitudes: 'We've actually just bought an Avid, which is becoming a necessity for off-line' (Phil Stone); 'We bought it because it was a facility we needed to offer to our clients. We thought it was a good idea to offer off-line' (Andrew Coppin), a feeling shared by small owner-operated facilities. 'There would be a certain number of clients who had a favourite on-line suite and that suite did not yet have non-linear but they wanted to do their programme on non-linear' (Neil Roberts). And while they currently feel that 'a facility company is better off than a production company – we're able to more or less guarantee that it's working full time' (Bryn Roberts), there is a move towards programme production companies buying their own.

Individual production companies see the equipment as a just affordable tool: 'How many programmes, how many weeks? Four weeks editing of thirteen shows equals fifty-two weeks editing. It's a simple calculation – fifty-two weeks editing. Do we buy? At the end of the year we won't have recouped the full costs but if it's 75 per cent paid for it's worth going for' (Mike Whittaker), and dry-hire editing companies that specialise in off-line equipment feel that common attitudes in the industry require them to provide the latest generation of equipment so that their clients may satisfy *their* clients: 'Our

16

market is the editors not the production companies. Really get to the niche–bottom line if we keep the editors happy then they'll bring their clients' (Charles Lennard).

Throughout the industry, only a few individuals feel that non-linear editing is not a 'sea change' in editing technology and working practices. All other sectors are convinced that it is here to stay.

Note

1. *Nonlinear: A Survey from the User's Point of View*, Research conducted between 1 June to 1 October 1992, (London: SYPHA Consultants, November 1992).

THE PROGRAMMES

Non-linear systems are not particularly suited to one programme type or another because of the way they operate. The most important limiting factor is the picture storage available for use on any given machine. Most systems *can* have very large amounts of storage available, but over four to five hours is currently prohibitively expensive. Also, loading the machine with rushes and unloading it afterwards must be done in real time. This can mean five hours to unload a machine to Exabyte storage tape to free it up for the next job. Incoming jobs must also allow for selection and storage or digitising of the rushes material before editing can begin: 'One of the things that they are finding from feedback they are getting is that some of the agencies are getting really pissed off because they are wanting to come in tomorrow to do something and the suite is saying, "Oh well your stuff's not on the system"' (David Archibald).

Figures are hard to come by, and of uncertain validity, but *Cuts*

Fig. 3

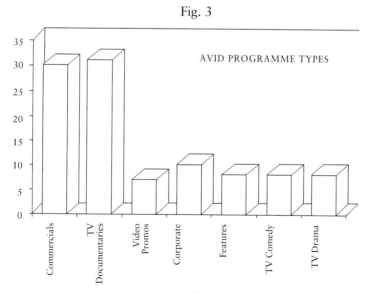

18

magazine (January 1993, p. 32) offered a survey of non-linear machines that showed the types of programme they were cutting (see fig. 3). These percentages were offered on a sample basis of only thirty-nine machines Europe-wide. Figures for Lightworks of documentaries (24 per cent), television drama (26 per cent), commercials (18 per cent) and corporate (11 per cent) come from '11 per cent of the user base'. Many people believe that Lightworks have delivered forty systems in the United Kingdom, and so 11 per cent of the UK-user base amounts to approximately four machines. Similarly, the report that 65–70 per cent of jobs cut on the EMC^2 are television documentaries is drawn from a base of only three machines of that type operating in the United Kingdom.

The type of work reported here may be a reflection of the type of work the purchaser was familiar with before his or her purchase, or may be as simple as one major contract that funded the purchase of the system. There are, however, several general principles that can be discerned: 'There are two sources of work – work that used to be done on off-line and work that used to be done on film. Thus for the first time non-linear editing has merged those two' (Bryn Roberts). Certainly, non-linear is regarded as an off-line format: 'If you're doing a one-hour documentary, you'd want to cut it first. Avid just makes it easier to do, that's all' (Bob Dowie). But off-line will include the most prestigious type of television drama that has the highest production values, and is destined to have a life beyond initial transmission in the library, together with prestige but fast throughput drama: 'It's cutting a six-part drama serial shot on Super 16. Sound is recorded on DAT. Future proofing.' (Neil Roberts); '*Casualty*, you know, on Saturday night – it's been a major electronic off-line on-line quick turn round success for us' (Neil Pittaway).

Despite some industry detractors: 'In film drama and news there's no movement towards Avid' (Bob Dowie), many people operating in precisely these areas feel that there is a definite advantage to programme production from non-linear editing. The BBC News and Current Affairs department is experimenting with a 'beta test' version of a non-linear machine that will transmit its results directly to air, but many regard the system's technical quality as being not quite ready yet: 'Where News have the advantage is that they're not constrained by, dare I say, technical quality' (Neil Pittaway). Nonetheless, this is still early days for non-linear news production, even if you accept that the necessary speed of their operation may allow shading of absolute technical standards. News works so fast that unless non-linear editing output can be transmission-ready, it will be of limited use: 'We have no NLE on daily output – we couldn't conform fast enough' (Ken Connell).

In general, non-linear is establishing itself as the preferred method of off-line editing. Programme-makers who had previously originated their programmes on film: 'A lot of people in this company have been loyal to film production on the documentary side because of the flexibility they've had in editing. What I'm seeing is now that people are getting the flexibility in editing on Avid plus a bit more, those people are now beginning to turn towards acquiring on tape' (John Surtees), turned to different origination mediums. When producers returned with the large amounts of material enabled by the low cost of video acquisition: 'We have had *Panoramas* with 170:1 shooting ratios' (Neil Pittaway), the storage problems became apparent. Programme producers are forced to preselect their material for the non-linear edit session. As long as this is possible, any programmes are suitable for non-linear editing.

There are reported uses of non-linear machines on location with complicated commercials[1] and feature films. But non-linear machines are making the biggest inroads into those areas of post-production that previously had an off-line component.

Note

1. Ariston multi-layer commercials transmitted 1992–3.

ADVANTAGES AND DISADVANTAGES

The main reason that non-linear editing has found such ready acceptance among editors is its ability to allow editors of material originated on any medium the flexibility that is associated with film editing. The restrictions imposed by linear video methods of editing have long been resented: 'When tape came in for the majority of television production, I think that programme craft skills went out of the window' (David Archibald). A common attitude about video machinery is: 'Don't worry me about the technology, Avids or things, it's what's on the screen that matters' (Neil Pittaway), and this is mirrored in the way the manufacturers refer to their products: 'The Steenbeck style is . . . an implicit part of what Lightworks is' (Trevor Morecraft); 'Film editors tend to like using Optima because they say "at last I don't have to worry about anything to do with video; I can just look at pictures and cut"' (Charles Lennard).

Not only do the editors like the new systems for the freedom they have reintroduced to picture editing: 'It's so natural because it's so much like a film operation' (David Archibald); 'It was brilliant. It did exactly what it was supposed to do' (Bob Dowie), but the process is faster: 'A thirty-minute programme in three days and that was just 9.30–5.30. Staggering. We then spent another three days tweaking' (Keith Oliver); 'It's something that on a film edit would have been a six-week schedule per programme and we're doing it in ten days. You couldn't do it on tape. Absolutely not – there's just no way' (David Archibald), and a programme that is cut faster, but with no quality loss through haste, is a better production.

The high cost of non-linear editing means that 'There's a fine line on whether you can justify it on a cost basis. I can definitely justify it on a decision basis – the options it gives when you're on a programme-making basis you can't deny; it's absolutely fantastic' (Keith Oliver); 'It's going to be quicker but it's not going to be any cheaper' (Bryn Roberts); 'Any savings are in terms of time, not quality' (Peter Marshall), *but* significant sums of money can be saved in final editing or conforming: 'I can guarantee to halve an on-line normally, and if I run the list, I'll quite often do that in an evening or overnight' (David

Archibald). Some facility houses like 'The Mill' in London are opening on-line suites that are aimed specifically at gathering non-linear auto-conform business.

All sides are keen to stress that non-linear editing is a creative method first and foremost: 'I don't want to sell it on speed, I want to sell it on the quality of the end product' (David Archibald), but it is undoubtedly true that 'providing you put a disciplined producer with a disciplined editor and a very disciplined time scale and a limited budget, and all those things together, you're going to win' (Neil Pittaway); 'It can be a way of containing production costs' (Peter Marshall).

And as with good things that seem to be all advantages, there is another side to the coin – a price to pay: 'The suppliers are just controlling the industry' (Bryn Roberts), although the manufacturers argue that their system prices reflect the high cost of storage peripherals and other major capital equipment parts, and are similar across non-linear manufacturers. It is undoubtedly true that the high cost of systems, and in particular storage, have a significant impact on the development of the sector: 'You want a Betacam and an Avid and transfer as you go. But you run into major storage problems very quickly' (Neil Pittaway). The initial price is a hurdle large enough to deter new entrants to the sector – 80 per cent of respondents to the SYPHA survey stated cost as the first reason for not investing in a non-linear system,[1] but even those who are committed are concerned about the cost: 'I mean, I spent nine or ten months thinking very carefully about investing in one of these things because it's a lot of dosh, especially just doing it myself. The downtime costs of a Lightworks or Avid are quite high' (David Archibald); 'I did a study about six months ago about setting up a company with two Avids – a stand-alone company – and I could see no way of making any money at all' (Phil Stone). The cost of the equipment also hinders the industry from seeing the non-linear sector as a viable off-line area: 'You see an Avid or Lightworks and they are brilliant. It's great but is it an off-line cost? If you've got a commercials' budget maybe, but if you've got broadcast work I can't see how it pays' (David Archibald).

The high initial cost of the systems inevitably means that owners have less storage than they would ideally like. This impacts on the rigour of preselection of rushes, the time taken for digitising and the time taken to unload the machines to Exabyte tapes. Currently, machines that use magneto-optical technology for picture storage are not constrained directly in this fashion, but this type of storage has its own limitations: 'The editing's a doddle. It's the management aspects of non-linear that are difficult' (David Archibald).

The speed with which the systems work creates new pressures. Typically, a non-linear editor will be able to follow the director's cutting order and amendments with great speed, so much so that a director who might previously have had to wait for a video editor to execute a complicated edit will find the edit performed and the editor and system standing by for the next decision almost instantly. Similarly, the editors have less time for pause: 'I find it quite tiring as well. You're never actually laying anything down. You're never actually sitting there while you copy twenty seconds' worth nor can you say, "that bit's done" ' (Keith Oliver).

While automation of repetitive parts of the editing procedure is practicable, the area is so complex that it can cause problems: 'When you get an edit list that's come in off somebody who doesn't understand the Lightworks which they've hired for two days, and they've got into the files and all the other things and made a right mess of it, somebody's got to be in a position to understand that mess and unscramble it' (Neil Pittaway); 'We've had some programmes on it that have caused us a lot of problems' (Bob Dowie). But while software problems and operating practices can be attended to, the cost of the systems remains a barrier to very rapid expansion of this sector of the industry. A question about future purchases elicited a cautious response: 'The cost cannot be justified at the moment' (Keith Oliver); 'The Avid 2000 is really too expensive for the job it's doing and we're looking to buy more systems; we're looking at the cheaper-end Lightworks' (Ken Connell); 'It's whether Lightworks could ever pay for itself and I still don't see the sums adding up' (David Archibald).

Notes

1. *Nonlinear: A Survey from the User's Point of View*, Research conducted between 1 June to 1 October 1992, (London: SYPHA Consultants, 1992), p. 51.

THE EDITORS

The wide penetration of non-linear editing into off-line areas is matched by the sources of non-linear editors: 'They've come from one of the traditional routes and attached the Avid' (John Surtees), although there seems to be a natural affinity between the craft skills learned by film editors and the disciplines of editing non-linear: 'They have a slightly better innate understanding of what editing non-linear means' (Charles Lennard); 'Film editors who've worked in the business for over twenty-five years switched to Avid and were very familiar with Avid in two weeks – they love it as well. They really like it' (Mike Whittaker); 'A lot of our clients who are film editors but doing commercials mainly, are bringing in Avid or Lightworks discs that we conform to' (Phil Stone).

Editors who learned their skills on videotape bring different skill advantages to non-linear editing: 'I think it's very important that an off-line editor or non-linear editor should be able to do the on-line as well' (Phil Stone), as one of the often quoted reasons for installation of non-linear machines is to feed a facility house's on-line suite: 'All the jobs we've taken on non-linear have gone through our on-line' (Keith Oliver).

The editors themselves look favourably on the new technology, and do not see it as a threat: 'I went into non-linear so that I could get back to editing the way I like to edit' (David Archibald); 'The Avid editors don't see themselves as anything special or better. It's considered as a natural progression of the editing job' (John Surtees). Rather, they regard the skills as an extra string to their bow in the increasingly competitive field of television post-production: 'I can learn one of these non-linear editing systems and have something existing editors don't have' (Charles Lennard).

Unsurprisingly, editors all felt that non-linear systems should be operated by editors, for the benefit of the creative integrity of the programme. Despite the ease of operation of the machines: 'To actually get the basics of joining shots together takes about two hours' (David Archibald), there is doubt that those without considerable experience of the visual grammar of programme production will be able to edit satisfactorily: 'The way we recruit picture editors – we are looking for a high degree of editorial awareness and journalistic qualities. Visual literacy is taken for granted' (Ken Connell); 'Basically the situation is that a few myths have sprung up around non-linear. The first is that it is so easy to use you don't need an editor' (Neil Roberts); 'What remains to be seen is whether a director has that editing skill or whether he needs to rely on a craftsman who can interpret his overall wish' (Peter Marshall).

While there was some dissension, there was general agreement that the editor is more than an operator and adds an extra creative layer to the programme: 'We very much think that the technology, whether it's tape, non-linear or anything else is not irrelevant, but first and foremost people buy people' (Charles Lennard); 'Editing is an eye, it's rhythm, it's partly something you're born with' (Neil Roberts).

Existing editors are keen to acquire the new skills, and in their efforts to obtain conversion training encounter different attitudes. Large employers that pay for the training of their own staff, both in cash and time lost from work, are reluctant to convert their editors unless there is an immediate and defined need: 'Everybody wants an Avid course. Fine, but the chances of you seeing an Avid in the next twelve months are extremely remote. We've got one officially' (Ken Connell).

Equipment manufacturers are keen to expand the base of editors who are familiar with their brand of non-linear editor. Stories abound of numbers of machines 'on loan' to broadcasters, and manufacturers will let editors familiarise themselves on their equipment free of charge: 'We have never ever charged to train an editor on anything. We have spent incalculable hours teaching people how to use things like Shotlister' (Charles Lennard). Production and facility companies with their own non-linear systems will frequently let their stable of freelance editors have access to the machines in 'downtime' – an arrangement in which both parties benefit, as there is no cash outlay from either side. It is of course an unreliable method of skills conversion, but can be a useful source of editors due to the short period required for already skilled editors to learn non-linear skills. What will be much harder to develop will be the *next* generation of editors as changes in working practices may lead to the redundancy of assistant editors.

CHANGES IN WORKING PRACTICES

Visual literacy, both acquired and developed, remains at the heart of editing, no matter what the technological tool. Other things are also unchanged. Cutting rooms remain darkened rooms, with flickering screens. Editors spend many hours a day cut off from daylight, and frequently from fresh air also. Lightworks have considered ergonomic factors in the design of their machines: 'The colours we use on the graphics monitor have been carefully chosen as fairly soft and gentle pastel shades because we recognise that people are going to have to sit in front of this unit for *twelve to fifteen hours a day* [my italics] and we want to cut the eye strain. We believe that one of the advantages of us only having one screen [is that] you're not moving your eye muscles or neck muscles to move your vision between screens' (Trevor Morecraft).

I did not find any complaints about design features that led to any identifiable repetitive strain injuries (RSI), but undoubtedly general principles associated with health and safety when working with computers would apply. In many respects, however, non-linear systems are likely to be much less of a problem than general, intensive computer use. Editors interact with the machine by means of a keyboard and a mouse, allowing a less intensive series of actions. Further, success does not depend on a high rate of key strokes; frequently the reverse is true, with pause and consideration being valued.

Nonetheless, the introduction of non-linear editing has caused some changes in editing philosophy and working practice. An example of this change is the lack of a physical programme at the end of a non-linear session. You can copy a visual reference of the edit onto videotape for viewing elsewhere but 'The thing we always try to ram home to people is that they're not producing an off-line edited tape, they're producing a floppy disc, because that's what matters at the end of the day. Whatever appears on the screen is a representation of the floppy disc. Virtual editing' (Andrew Coppin).

This fundamental change in the end result of the editing process also makes changes at the outset of the editing process, with rushes logging. All the material for a non-linear edit must be placed into the system's database by a digitising process. As storage is limited – largely by price – a preselection must be made. If the log of shots is prepared on a suitably compatible database, then not only do you have the information in a form that is readily accessible to the non-linear operator, but the same database can be used to instruct the non-linear machine to select material for digitising, and 'The editor, once he had digitised the stuff into the machine, could do a rough cut from the database. You can bolt the rough cut together in less than the running time of the programme' (Neil Roberts); 'I mean, you're storyboarding it on the non-linear – a sequence of shots basically' (Neil Pittaway).

With the spread of powerful portable computers, this editing log will increasingly be created outside the cutting room: 'You've got a time code generator in the camera and we're working on systems that will transmit that time code into the Psion on site. Right away you've built up a pretty sophisticated list' (Neil Pittaway). This list, with comments from the production staff on location, will instruct the non-linear machine exactly which shots to digitise and may even per-form a first assembly with minimal human intervention. While this is technically possible already, its spread will be limited because 'There's a whole range of concepts there that means we've got to have similar language inputting and outputting to these devices' (Neil Pittaway). Until this becomes a standard across the industry, detailed logging will still probably be carried out in the cutting room. Certainly editors think so at the moment: 'It's got a built-in assistant, but somebody's got to log the shots' (David Archibald). Creation of a suitable log while shooting will soon be the norm, but until this is so, assistant editors have a place in the cutting room: 'I have put one assistant between two Avids and basically they just do the housekeeping. The role they have is very much of a film assistant in terms of co-ordinating the material and the organisation' (John Surtees).

The editing process itself is transformed. To extend a shot or sequence, or to move that same section to another part of the pro-gramme, is a matter of moments. If the director wants to see a differ-ent version, the material does not have to be copied or recut – merely replayed from the database store in different orders. Artistic decisions are enabled because it is so easy to make changes, and any changes do not take significant amounts of costly time or materials. Also, even the simplest professional non-linear systems have four soundtracks available for editing use. This is a significant advance for non-film editing – easily accessible places to put programme sound. Sound-tracks are laid up in the same manner as film, during and immediately after the picture edit and could be done by a trainee editor: 'There is a role there for an assistant. I have not quite worked out what it is, but I think it's at the end of the off-line process' (Mike Whittaker). Currently, there is often a pre-edit for sound alone in the on-line suite: 'The main problem with non-linear systems at the moment is transporting all that beautiful track-laying information to the dubbing suite' (David Archibald). But as common standards develop, and new machines that are capable of performing sound mixing within the non-linear machine itself become more common, all sound information created in the non-linear edit will be instantly transferable to the sound mixing suite. When this happens, unless a specialist, non-linear dubbing editor grade develops, the picture editor will have attended to the sound without the need for an assistant.

Film programmes and programmes originated on videotape have copies made for loading the non-linear machine, and the masters are stored: 'Invariably we do a duplex record onto D1 and Betacam for Avid users' (Phil Stone). After the non-linear edit, the final edit is frequently auto-conformed to match the non-linear EDL with minimal human intervention. Currently, about 80 per cent of the length of most programmes edited on a non-linear machine is auto-conformed in this fashion, with significant time and cost savings. The remaining 20 per cent, which has titles and more complicated visual effects, is completed conventionally. However, as the non-linear machines develop, it will be possible to achieve complete auto-conform on-line edit of the most complicated programmes from a non-linear EDL, and on-line editors will become a disappearing breed as auto-conforming increases in competence.

The traditional areas of picture editing that have required assistant editors are disappearing. Logging will not be done in the cutting room, tape handling will be minimal in the cutting room, sound will have, at best, a small labour requirement. Even film negative cutting will be affected as non-linear editors with film masters will produce frame-accurate negative cutting lists that have worked-out optical dissolve overlays and potential double use of frames.

Currently there is a belief that assistants are necessary: 'The thing that is coming through is that Avid needs an assistant' (Bob Dowie); 'I bring in a lot of assistants now, freelance assistants to work on Avid' (John Surtees), but many feel that as the technology develops 'we won't have the assistant level' (Bryn Roberts). Certainly, while the editing process itself has been vastly improved, the peripheral tasks have been, and are being, removed from the cutting room. While some of these tasks are sheer drudgery and should go, they provided avenues for the employment and training of the next generation of editors.

WHENCE NEW EDITORS?

The equipment and originating mediums of film and videotape have always called for editors to have support. Assistant editors managed the cutting rooms, leaving the editors free to concentrate on the pictures: 'Every suite has an assistant editor. He's actually sitting in the edit suite. This is a very important relationship' (Phil Stone); 'The way the BBC worked in the old days, there were always two people involved in the edit. An editor and assistant, even on the videotape side' (Keith Oliver).

Custom and practice allowed completely unskilled recruitment, and learning on the job: 'They start as runners and go into the machine room loading tapes, assisting' (Phil Stone); 'There is only one way to learn to edit, you've got to get behind the master and watch' (Neil Pittaway). However, the changes in working practices concomitant with the shift to non-linear editing do not allow for a paid but non-skilled person in the cutting room: 'The whole non-linear thing is going to be the cause of a problem for the industry in that where does the next generation of editors come from? Arguably, you don't need an assistant editor in a non-linear suite' (Trevor Morecraft); 'The only way you can learn to be an editor is to sit at somebody's elbow for five or six years, and that's really not going to happen. I don't know what the answer is' (Mike Whittaker); 'There's no room for assistants and no room for anybody to learn' (David Archibald).

Everybody surveyed accepted the emergence of the problem: 'Certainly if I believe that there is a skills gap emerging, which I believe there is anyway, then I'd want to do something about it. But how I'd do it, I don't know' (John Surtees); 'It's certainly a major problem. I don't know what I can do to help. I've been trying to find a role for assistants' (Mike Whittaker).

While there is uncertainty about the action to be taken, there is agreement about the skills needed. The technology is comparatively transparent to the user, and will become more so. The valuable skill will be visual literacy: 'I believe that editing is about timing, it's about joining pictures together, it's about constructing what goes on the screen' (Neil Pittaway), but if working practices do not allow the acquisition of this skill by observation: 'There is, as far as I can see, very little area for learning the skill of cutting pictures any more' (Keith Oliver), how are the new generation of editors to learn? 'Perhaps the industry should consider that sooner or later there are going to have to be two people in every non-linear suite because you're going to need to have a junior trainee in there to replace the guy that's driving it at the front end' (Trevor Morecraft).

However, a second crew member in the cutting room, superficially with little direct productivity benefit, is expensive. Some feel that an assistant is as necessary as ever, and persuade their customers: 'What I'm doing is getting the producers to pay for them. I'm saying here's the rate and this job requires an assistant to get it done in the time you want' (David Archibald); 'I've just talked to a customer about Avid and downloading, and was trying to persuade her to use an assistant for four hours a day, twenty hours a week' (Bob Dowie), but a direct cost/benefit ratio is never far from their minds: 'I have to operate very much within a means to an end here. I've got bottom lines, I've got targets to meet. I've got facilities to run. I've always said that although I'm totally in favour of training and retraining, I'm not doing training for training's sake' (John Surtees); 'I won't train anyone that I don't have to train' (Bob Dowie). And others do not feel that training is their responsibility at all: 'I consider training important, but when we set up the company we went for the best sound man in the BBC, the best VT editor in the BBC in Cardiff, the best two VT editors from HTV, the best two film editors from the BBC. We do see that there is a need to train, but it's very difficult to get a client to train' (Bryn Roberts); 'If we had a rotating pool of trained assistants we'd be jolly happy to plug into that' (Mike Whittaker); 'I do not see it as part of my business to train editors unless the right person was in the right place at the right time' (Andrew Coppin).

Even when training is seen as necessary, it is not offered as part of general skill raising, only as reaction to a specific need: 'I don't see the point of giving somebody a week's training on Avid if he's not going to use it for the following year' (Bob Dowie); "The thing we find about training on specific equipment is that unless you start using it the next week it's mostly wasted' (Ken Connell). Even those people and organisations that are prepared to train find themselves operating in a new culture that places a lower priority on training for the future: 'At the moment we're going through bad times and cutting staff, but it will hopefully bottom out and we'll be back into the recruitment business. Financial constraints are bound to creep in here. But if we said we're not going to do this any more we might as well shut up shop and go tomorrow because where would we get our people from?' (Neil Pittaway).

Apart from those few who were prepared to take on an assistant in the non-linear cutting room, there was little agreement about the best way to train non-linear editors from scratch: 'I don't think an editor, whether they started in film or video or start in non-linear or anything else, should be trained initially in anything else than the grammar of joining shots together' (Neil Pittaway). Allowing people the time to learn visual literacy: 'It takes two to seven years depending on where you're trying to get them to train' (Neil Pittaway), is a luxury that few were prepared to offer commercially, and many offered the opinion that 'to acquire visual literacy, I guess it has to be the existing generation of training institutions – if there is not the facility within industry then it has to be found in colleges or whatever' (Andrew Coppin). This is partly a reluctance by an increasingly pressured industry to increase the cost burden of training on thinning profit margins, but is also partly a hope that a democratisation process will allow new blood to emerge: 'Now we can walk down to Dixons and buy an edit controller, a caption generator, a camera that's almost broadcast quality and the whole lot for under £5,000. The whole thing has become casualised – democratised. That's good and bad. You get a lot of people thinking they're movie-makers now' (John Surtees); 'To me the great hope is that now these little 8mm video recorders are around and that people who wouldn't normally make movies are going to be making them . . . the professionalism about movies will be destroyed for ever and it will become an art form';[1] 'I would like to see people coming out of colleges with show reels that they've cut on Lightworks, or whatever, which break all the rules and create whole new styles of editing which work' (Neil Roberts).

The colleges that are being put in the position of providers may not have to buy leading-edge technology from tight education budgets. Non-linear manufacturers have informal arrangements with some of the colleges for the provision of access to machines, to produce craftspeople familiar with one particular type of system to enhance sales potential: 'At any one time we have about seven Bournemouth film school people' (Charles Lennard), and this education and training does not need to be done on state-of-the-art non-linear technology: 'What you will see is that more and more of the colleges and film schools will adopt non-linear as part of the process at our level. However, the non-linear concept can be just as well demonstrated by a simple Apple system as by a full-blown Lightworks system' (Trevor Morecraft).

Throughout the industry there is an acceptance of the fact that while existing editors can be cross-trained into non-linear editors with relative ease, unless new editors are given the chance to spend a considerable amount of time watching and living with pictures, and being allowed to experiment, there will be no method of training that the industry can offer in any depth to ensure the supply of new editors. There is no substitute for time spent watching and performing edits, good edits, bad edits, in existing programmes and in trial programmes. If new edit suites do not need assistants, the only way we can ensure a supply of new blood is to provide a framework in which people can be exposed to large amounts of pictures, possibly with formal instruction. While some visual literacy is innate, perhaps film schools and colleges are a natural place to acquire this skill?

Note

1. Francis Ford Coppola, *Hearts of Darkness*, television documentary, 1982. 1st UK TX BBC 2, March 1993.

TRENDS

In a sector of the industry that is changing as fast as the non-linear area, predictions are often outdistanced by reality. However, some trends are clear: 'I don't think that film will ever go, for a start' (Phil Stone); 'There will still be people shooting on film then in ten years' time. I am almost certain of it' . . . 'I suspect that we're looking at the last tape formats now, one of them D5 digital Betacam' (Neil Pittaway). Film and digital tapeless acquisition will be the future origination mediums. As non-linear editing continues to spread fast, this material will be cut on non-linear machines that *may* not be cheaper but will have much more storage: 'There are new optical drives coming out with no international standard as yet, but the picture quality will just take a magnitude leap forward' (Trevor Morecraft); 'Now there is a new optical disc development come along that's probably going to double the performance of optical discs in the next eighteen months, and at that time it's going to be very practical for us to start using optical discs as both a source and record machine' (David Archibald). Other views are that technological advances *will* result in cheaper systems: 'I'm sure that the price of professional systems is going to come down. And the professional systems will develop and become broadcast quality. For news and current affairs this year' (Bryn Roberts); 'In a couple of years I think first the price will be such that they'll just be buying a piece of software and another hard or optical disc to go with their existing computer system, so the chances are they'll buy it just like they'll buy a piece of word processing software or desk top publishing' (Charles Lennard).

Whether you believe that prices will come down or not, there is general agreement that the quality of the pictures will go up and soon reach broadcast quality on most machines. The amount of storage available will increase the range of programmes that can be edited on them: 'I can see that as soon as there is a broadcast quality non-linear system which can handle a ninety-minute football match, that a sports producer would just want to be able to do the same' (Neil Pittaway).

As the manufacturers are very responsive to the needs of the professional community, there will undoubtedly be major advances in the ability of non-linear machines to network with each other: 'We're looking for a non-linear broadcast system which is networkable. So material can be swapped around from terminal to terminal and will be used by multiskilled people. You'll have Newscutters cutting stories and dumping it to Airplay' (Ken Connell). The picture editors may well be journalists for many news and current affairs stories and single, assignable machines may be capable of many functions: 'The work station could be an off-line one day, a telecine one day, an on-line the next day, it could be a graphic station another day. Now you wouldn't ask one operator to do all those things' (Phil Stone). However, there is likely to remain 'a small core of specialist picture editors who will be there to do the stuff that needs a high craft skill' (Ken Connell).

CONCLUSION

The field of non-linear editing is currently small. There may be around one hundred and twenty sophisticated machines operating in the United Kingdom, contributing less than a thousand hours to the half a million or more programme hours produced annually by broadcasters, corporate users, cable and satellite channels. Two years ago, however, there were fewer than ten primitive machines in the United Kingdom.

As prices fall and the capability of non-linear machines increases, ownership will spread dramatically. There is widespread industry agreement that non-linear editing has significant advantages for programme production over *all* other methods of post-production for *all* origination methods. Currently, most machines are in use for broadcast programming, whether edited in broadcast companies or external facility houses. Ownership in these sectors will continue to increase, but dramatic growth will also be seen in the ownership of machines by small production companies, individual editors and corporate television producers, all of whom are currently inhibited by price. The cost of the systems is by far the largest restraining factor to explosive growth in the sector. Even at current prices, most owners are planning to at least *double* their non-linear capability in less than twelve months. Add all those individuals and companies who are about to purchase their first machine and exponential growth is certain.

There is no doubt that non-linear editing will be the preferred, if not the only, method of editing programmes within ten years. Programmes originated on film will be transferred to non-linear machines for the entire editing process, returning to the negative only for the final stages, perhaps not even then if high definition video copies are taken immediately after initial processing. Programmes originated on video will download their recordings – possibly directly from a solid state device – to the non-linear machine, and may not have any external processes at all thereafter. Completed programmes will be transmitted directly from networks of non-linear editors. Most of this is in operation now, or will be in months rather than years.

Film cutting rooms will disappear, together with film editors and assistant editors. Video on-line suites will shrink for most uses to auto-conforming suites. As non-linear editing power increases, conforming suites will perform more and more of the end stages automatically, and the final conform will soon be performed by the non-linear machine directly controlling conventional video machines. The skills of on-line editors will be gradually lost. Within ten years programmes will be completed and transmitted from the same machine, led by the field of news and current affairs. Programme graphics, already heavily computerised, and other specialist segments will be prepared elsewhere and networked into the non-linear machines. The non-linear editor will be the final creative layer in programme production and will not need an assistant to operate the machinery. Increases in machine power, storage and retrieval rates will reduce the amount of housekeeping to be done during a programme, and further reduce the need for an assistant.

Arguably, the current new generation of editors aged 25+ will be the last to have the traditional entry to, and training in, the industry – starting at the bottom and learning on the job. These 25-year-old editors may be expected to have a working life of at least thirty years ahead of them, and to convert them to non-linear editors is simple and cheap. They will postpone the imminent staffing crisis for some years, but their numbers will not be self-replacing as in the past, and will not be sufficient to allow the significant increase in numbers of non-linear machines to be operated by skilled and visually literate editors. There is likely to be a serious shortfall of specialist picture editors within ten years.

The industry as a whole is currently reluctant to train newcomers on expensive equipment, but as equipment costs come down some *may* be prepared to take on trainees. As costs come down, film schools and colleges will find themselves in an increasingly strategic position. They will be able to afford enough equipment to allow a high degree of student access, and colleges will provide one of the main sources of *time* for a new generation of editors to acquire visual literacy.

As the demand for trained staff increases, potential employees denied training will not be able to demonstrate the experience that is currently sought by those employers who will not train for themselves. There will be no need for a qualification in the operation of the machines, as within five years most school leavers will be conversant with the skills needed. Visual literacy or good editing is such a subjective area, it will be difficult to establish criteria for vocational qualifications.

Broadcasters will continue to provide a source of training in this area, but training costs will impact directly on profits, and profits will increasingly be the yardstick by which broadcasters are measured.

Consequently, training will slip down the agenda. Training is mostly viable as a medium-to long-term investment, and increasingly broadcasters and production companies, under pressure to perform in the short term, will not see this as one of their priorities.

If the technology becomes sufficiently cheap, programme production will become democratised in much the same way that computing has moved from special environments tended by a 'priesthood' of men in white coats to everybody's back bedroom. Editors, as well as camera people, producers, directors, and so on will emerge as their talent is enabled. Some of the best of these people will enrol in higher education courses to nurture their talent, and a lucky few will be taken on by large broadcasters. Graduates from these colleges will have the show reels required by prospective employers, and these allied with personal presentation will be crucial to their employment prospects. The remainder will be taken on by small production companies in their offices, or as general assistants on the basis of their home-made show reels. They will be given their breaks often because they happened to be there and were cheap.

As the industry is unlikely to train most of its own new blood given current attitudes, the burden of training replacement editors will fall increasingly on further and higher education colleges. They may not be able to satisfy industry demand for recruits with demonstrable experience, and in the absence of a widely recognised system of qualifications we can only hope that the democratising nature of the technology will allow fresh and natural new talent to emerge.

POSTSCRIPT

Since the report was researched in January and February 1993, the non-linear editing arena has continued to develop rapidly. Montage re-launched in March with a range of machines starting at under £20,000 including up to one hour's storage. DVision are the new image of TouchVision – another of the early pioneers of the 80s. Their new range of machines starts at under £14,000 including storage of up to four hours in standard configuration. The DVision machines are based around the new Intel/IBM chip set called Digital Video Interactive (DVI), which uses new compression methods delivering SVHS quality from high compression ratios. This compression system may replace MPEG and JPEG. Lightworks released a broadcast-quality machine – 'Heavyworks' – at Montreux in June and Avid's top range Media Composers now claim broadcast quality. Both the BBC and ITN have used Avid's 'Newscutter' for news items broadcast directly to air. All levels of machine will now output directly to discs suitable for PC multimedia applications.

Prices are dropping fast, quality is rising and competition is fierce. Avid claim to be selling twenty systems per month in the United Kingdom alone. DVision claim to have sold 900 systems worldwide since 1992. I estimate that over 500 systems will be sold in Britain alone in 1993. A far cry from the 1,800 systems sold worldwide between 1980 and 1992.

Primitive non-linear editing can now start at under £5,000 and professional systems start at £10,000. Top end systems, however, are still expensive at £70,000+. Production companies now see non-linear editing as a standard post-production path.

Despite the exponential growth in the sales of non-linear machines, training provision has not kept pace. The National Film and Television School and other leading film schools are offering courses to enable industry professionals to try and come to grips with the new technology, but there is still no substantial provision for the training of the new generation of picture editors.

As linear video technology is becoming obsolete and we are not developing new skills, we can still expect a shortage of skilled picture editors within eight years.

September 1993